More Than A Degree:

How to Get the Most out of College

By Samson Sembeba

More Than a Degree: How to Get the Most out of College
Published by Dale-Samson Ntihinyuka Sembeba.

Table of Contents

More Than A Degree

*As you embark on your journey through college, know that you are not alone. You walk with God; thus, you **<u>will</u>** leave a mark.*

Dedication

This book is dedicated to:

Natali Sembeba, my wife. Your love fuels me.

My Mom, Dad and Sister (Sage). You dealt with years of being separated from me because you believed in what God was doing in my life.

My Uncle (Francois Nambajimana, Muchachuman), for being the first author in our family and paving the way. RIP.

The faculty and staff of Great Lakes Adventist Academy. If it had not been for having the opportunity to serve the students on that campus, I would have not been prepared for college.

The faculty and staff that supported me at Southwestern Adventist University. If it had not been for your love and support, I wouldn't have had the confidence to serve at the university as I did.

The students who attended Southwestern Adventist University during Fall 2016 - Spring 2019. I appreciate the trust you gave me entering college, to serve in all the ways I did. If it had not been for all of you, I wouldn't have been prepared for the "real" world.

The friends that stuck after college and even before. The love and support you have given me helped me write this book.

The reader reading this book. If you are in college, don't hold back your God-given potential. Use it.

Introduction

I remember sitting in the office of Delwin Garcia, the principal at Great Lakes Adventist Academy, a boarding school in Cedar Lake, Michigan. I had been working at the Academy for two years now as a task-force dean and making stops into his office was always a joy for me. But this time it was a little different. This time going into his office, I did not realize I was going to receive something I was never going to let go of.

As we were talking, I mentioned how after working there for two years with the students, I felt like I knew how to get the most out of the boarding school experience. I can still remember the words flying out of my mouth: "I feel like if I went back in time to high school, I could succeed as a student and get the most out of this place." You see, I previously attended Great Lakes Adventist Academy as a student, and I was definitely not the greatest student. My grades were bad, and I cheated my way through every class. I didn't really have a walk with the Lord at all. I had a level of influence in the school, but I used it to do worse than good, and eventually the school saw me out the front door. Yes, that is code for "I got kicked out."

I know what you might be thinking. "If you got kicked out, how on earth did you end up working at the school as a task-force dean?" A year and a half after getting kicked out of the boarding academy, I had a near-death experience that made me take a fresh look at my faith. I decided I was going to go on a search for God for thirty days. After just a couple weeks, I saw my faith in a new light and I wanted to share it with everyone. I shared my testimony with students at different academies all over Michigan, and yes, that included the one I got kicked out of. After they examined my life and saw that I had really changed, they had an opening as a task-force dean and invited me to fill the position. God can do amazing things. Now, back to the topic of what I realized when talking to Delvin that day.

So, working at the Academy gave me some wisdom on how people can succeed, and get the most out of the boarding school experience. As a dean, I would spend late nights and early mornings talking to students about how to succeed in their schoolwork, how to leverage their jobs on campus, and about relationships, their spirituality, literally anything and everything in their lives. The best part is, I got to see them grow! After working there two years, I felt like I had found the secret to success. But being in that office talking to Delwin, I felt bummed that I wasn't able to build that time machine and go back to high school and redo my life. Have you ever felt like that before? Just bummed that God doesn't send you back in time to give you a chance to right some wrongs?

Well, that day Delwin Garcia told me something that I believe was God speaking to me. Delwin's response to my statement was, "Well, Samson, you know, this coming fall you have a chance to put everything into practice that you have learned and test it out." My mind was officially blown. Some of you are like, *Wait, wait! I didn't get it.* Let me break it down for you.

Before this conversation, I had decided that I was going to go to Southwestern Adventist University (SWAU) down in Keene, Texas, to study theology. This was a school that was over 1,000 miles from my home and the crazy part was I knew absolutely no one down there. I was going to attend a school where I didn't know a soul! Maybe that is your experience? Going somewhere that you are scared and afraid, where you do not know a single person. And I had been talking about how I was nervous, and I didn't know how I would do out there, but this day the game completely changed. Because a boarding academy is so close to the way college works, I knew I could transfer many ideas from my time at the academy to attending SWAU.

No longer was it just about me attending school in Texas, it was now bigger than that. It was me going out there to see if the tools I learned at Great Lakes Adventist Academy as a task-force dean were really going to work. I was more excited than ever to go to college now, because it felt like this was my time machine. And that is the beauty of God, He finds ways to give us second chances, even when we think all hope is lost.

A you read through this book you will notice two things. The first is that attaining or succeeding at anything is not easy, it's hard. If anyone tries to give you the shortcut to something, don't follow. Instead, trust the long road, the tough road. It's like climbing up a mountain; there may be ways to make it a smoother journey, but there are no shortcuts it is either run or walk up the mountain. This book is about making our journey smoother and getting the most we can out of college.

The second thing you'll see is that when you begin to look closely at the experiences I share, you will soon realize that everything that I did in my "second chance" was not extremely perfect. As a matter of fact, I made a lot of mistakes that I wish I could redo now. But the beauty of this is that God is teaching me that the mistakes that we make are opportunities for learning for the future, if not for ourselves, then to help someone else, and if not in the situation where we messed up, then for sure in the situations to come.

With all of that said, now is the time to jump In and see how the journey continues.

1

Running with Your Head Up!

When I was going through high school there was a class that I dreaded. The class for me was chemistry. Maybe some of you have a class like this.. You might be able to relate, or maybe you love chemistry—and if you do, you have a gift, cherish it. But chemistry was a dreadful class for me. I will never forget the teacher that taught the class. His name was Mr. Carter. He is one of the smartest people I have ever met and at the same time, he looked like he fought bears for fun.

Starting off in the chemistry class, I already saw myself slipping behind and like any great student, I resorted to the one thing that I knew might be able to save the day for me: cheating. Sadly, what was embarrassing was even through all the cheating I still ended up finding a way to fail that class. That also might be a situation you have found yourself in before.

For years I tried to just convince myself that chemistry was something that was not for me! We all say it, there is a class out there that we really don't like and so we say that that particular class isn't for me, or we don't like it, or we don't have that gene. Whichever way you put it, we all have that class. English? Math? Sciences? Which class is the one that you dread?

I remember coming to the doors of college and sitting down with my advisor. I will never forget what she told me. "Samson, it looks like you have to take a science class. Chemistry is open this semester!" I sat there and thought for a second. I realized this was my opportunity to face a fear I had been running from. I had just given my life to God during this time frame and I was sitting there consulting with God, wondering if this would be the best choice.

I like to take the easy route, but that day I was really struggling because something in me was telling me that it was possible, and if I gave chemistry another chance I would be blown away. As I looked back at the advisor, I told her, "Sign me up!" Now I remember this being one of those things that you say, and then you get really sick to your stomach afterwards. I was really about to take another class in a subject that I had failed, even with cheating. But something told me that it was going to be different this time around because I had God on my side. There is a Bible verse that I thought about a lot during this time, "For as he thinketh in his heart, so is he."

This means that whatever we think about in our life, that is what our lives seem to reflect. You think that you are bad in math. As long as you believe that, you will be bad in math. Same goes for English class, history class, and yes, chemistry class. I remember telling myself that I would have to go into this class with confidence.

I walked into the class and I went straight up to the teacher. I told her, "Hi, my name is Samson, and I am going to get an A in your class." She looked at me and said, "Okay?" with a puzzled expression on her face. Maybe too much confidence? I wouldn't recommend going up to your teacher and saying that—but I wouldn't recommend not doing it. By the end of the semester, I ended up getting one of the highest grades in the class.

I know what you might be thinking. *How?* Or maybe you might be thinking, *Well, you had it in you all along, but I don't because my situation is different.* But the question that I believe will help answer those questions is this: What makes my situation different from the first time I took the class?

I want you to imagine that you are running a race. And you are told that this race is going to be hard, very hard. As a matter of fact, you are told that other people have failed. And as you begin this race, you are starting off discouraged and begin running with your head down. You come up to this wall, your first obstacle. The wall seems too large to climb, so then you give up. But the thing is, if you had been running with your head up, you would have noticed that the wall was short enough for you to climb over. End of story.

When it comes to really anything in life, the question is: Are you running with your head down or your head up? We are human. We love challenge, we love obstacles, but we will never be champions if we have our heads down.

Why did I struggle the first time I took chemistry? Because I had my head down. I thought it was hard. I thought that it was impossible. I thought of the other people who have tried and failed. I thought of the tough teacher. I thought the walls that I encountered along the way were impossible for me to climb.

What brought me success the second time I took the class? I went in with my head high up! I thought I could do it. I thought it was possible. I thought of the people who have succeeded and that I was one of them. I thought about how the teacher was there for my success and not for my failure. I thought every wall I come up against I can climb over, and that the obstacles can be conquered.

What are you thinking about the classes that you are taking in college? This lesson doesn't just apply to classes; it can really apply to anything in life! It can be about sports, music, making friends, succeeding in a project you want to do. What is it for you? Are you running with your head down? Or are you running with your head up?

How to run with your head up

1. Ask yourself what assumptions have you made about yourself, based on a past situation? *(Assumptions like: I am bad at math, I can't make friends, I have no gifts or talents)*

2. Now I want you to try to envision yourself being good at or succeeding in whatever it was that came to you in the first question. *(What color shirt are you wearing as you succeed, what do the people around you look like? Really get a vivid picture.)*

3. Now try proclaiming the Bible verse, Philippians 4:13 over what you answered for question number one. Do you believe that God can help you to be good at it and succeed?

2

Be Uncomfortable for the Comfort of Others

Arriving on the campus of Southwestern Adventist University, I was very uncomfortable. I mean, this was not your ordinary uncomfortable, like your mom or dad showing baby pictures to your significant other uncomfortable; this is more.

Just picture it. I am a guy who drove all the way from Kalamazoo, Michigan, to a little town called Keene, Texas. I don't know a single person at this school, and I have no idea what Texas is even like. Literally all I imagined was people walking around in cowboy boots and hats—and there is nothing wrong with that, just a little different than Michigan. When I arrived on the campus, everyone looked really intimidating, the buildings looked taller than the buildings I was used to in high school. I drove in around 10 at night and all I could think was, "This is the place, I guess" in the most terrified internal voice possible.

I know what some of you who know me might be thinking. Aren't you an extrovert, Samson? For those who don't know me, yes, I am an extrovert. On the Myers-Briggs personality test, I scored a 98% in extroversion.

Growing up, I moved to different locations throughout my school years, attending 10 different schools, elementary throughout high school alone. My parents were nurses, so they found jobs everywhere. Being the "new kid," I was often bullied at school. This may be why new environments have always made me nervous, especially places where I knew I was going to be there for more than a year, because that meant I had to deal with the bullying for that time frame.

So, when I arrived on the college campus, I was right off the bat scared of all that could or couldn't happen. Starting off at my new school, I had the privilege of working for the Spiritual Life and Development Office. I will never forget the words of the man who was in charge of the place, Pastor Russ.

While giving the team our pep talk before the school year started, he said something that I still carry with me today. "Guys, our job is to be uncomfortable so that others can be comfortable." That was it! The job of a leader. The job of a person wanting to make a difference in the lives of other people. The way to making friends, the way to leaving a positive impression on people you meet.

Now you might be thinking, *That sounds super cool, like a quote from a movie, but what does that actually mean?* Well, I am glad that you asked! When it comes to interacting with people there is this awkward moment that we experience right before we actually "interact." You might have experienced this at the store, in the library, in class, on campus, or maybe even with a family member that you haven't officially met yet. It's the moment right before you say hello, or right before a possible interaction. What each person is usually thinking is, "Is this person going to talk to me?" "Are we about to interact?" or even maybe "I hope this person says something, because I don't know what to say."

The truth of the matter is that people don't like those moments. What Pastor Russ was trying to get through to us is, you be uncomfortable, so that they can be comfortable to respond. Go up to the person who is sitting by themselves, so that they don't have to come up to you. Wave and say hello to the person walking on the sidewalk, so they don't have to initiate the wave to you. Don't be afraid to be uncomfortable in order to allow the other person to be comfortable.

What I came to realize after implementing this, is that a college campus is the best place to practice being uncomfortable, especially in the beginning of the school year. People want to meet people in college: no one goes into college saying, "I've made all the friends that I want and I don't want any more." No! Not at all. People are more than ready to meet other people and connect and grow in relationships, but—and there is always that but, right?—everyone tends to lean on the side of shy, not wanting to be the one who goes out of their comfort zone.

As soon as I learned this, I began to go throughout the campus and anytime I had one of those "awkward" moments, or I saw someone by themselves, I would just say to them, "Hi my name is Samson, what's yours?" Then I would ask what their major is, where they were from and share with them my own major and hometown. When I did this, something amazing happened.

This huge place that seemed so scary and made me nervous all of a sudden became smaller and smaller, because I wasn't afraid to be uncomfortable to help others to be comfortable. And I carry that wherever I go, to the store, and even in my current profession. It takes the awkward situations and puts you in control, because before you have even met anyone, you have decided that you are going to go up to them and say something.

Towards the end of my time at SWAU, I would walk the campus literally saying hello to everyone. I'm not saying you have to do that, especially if you are a little more introverted. To be honest, there will be times when people aren't extremely responsive to you being the bigger person to be uncomfortable for their comfort. But I remind myself that I gave that person an opportunity and they had the choice about how to respond. If we remain silent in those times, we never give that person a chance.

While I was on the campus, there was this one girl that I would say hello to all the time. For some reason I would see her in the cafe, and in the library and just walking to class. So I would just wave and say hello— something I did to everyone. and she would just look at me and not say anything. But after a while, one day she smiled back and said hello.

One day we ran into each other at a program on campus and I just had to ask her, "Why did it take you so long to respond to my hello?" And what she told me was something I'll never forget. She said, "I didn't know if you were just being nice or if you actually wanted to be my friend." The uncomfortableness for some months led to a friendship.

Are you willing to be uncomfortable? This is something that helps not just on college campuses but anytime we are interacting with people. There are times I meet people and they think that I am this confident guy, but in reality I am just willing to be uncomfortable. And, get this: eventually, it actually becomes comfortable.

Ways to be uncomfortable for others to be comfortable

1. Say hello strictly to the people that you see in the library. Libraries tend to be semi-friendly areas on campus.
2. Say hello to people that you walk past on the sidewalk.
3. Offer to sit next to someone who is sitting by themselves in the cafeteria.
4. Next time you are sitting next to someone, ask them 3 questions. Ask them for their name, their major and where they are from. *(And make sure to share your information with them as well.)*
5. Give fist bumps to people in your class.

3

Build a Foundation of Questions

I remember when I officially wanted to become a pastor. I was super excited to tell everyone that I came in contact with that I finally know what I want to do with my life. I felt called and I felt excited at the same time, which is an awesome mix. You probably feel that way going into college, or going into a job on campus. Or maybe you don't know what to do yet—if that is you, don't worry. It is coming!

One thing kept happening as I would bring it up. Everyone would mention to me, "Oh no! That means you have to do Greek and Hebrew!" Literally people would tell me, "Good luck with that!" and they would paint this dark picture of what this class was going to look like, and it made me more nervous by the day. Why do people have to come and squash our excitement with news like that? But they do.

I knew the class was going to be hard, but I decided that I was going to keep my head up high! I knew that if I was working alongside God, then everything would work itself out.

But don't get me wrong, a hard class is not all just about prayer. There is no easy route to anything. It is all about prayer and hard work, that combination I knew was going to set me over the top! There is a quote that I love from one of my favorite authors, Ellen White. She says, "Prayer and effort, effort and prayer, this will be the business of our life. We must work as though the success is on us but pray knowing it's on Him."

I walked into the professors office and I remember him standing there with a blank look on his face when I asked him the question, "What do I have to do to succeed in Greek class?" If anyone knows how to pass the class, it should be the teacher. You would imagine that he would give me this long list, but instead of the long list, he gave me three things to do: read the chapter before class, attend class, and do your homework.

After hearing those words I jotted them down and headed out. Greek became one of the easiest classes that I had running off of that information. I never missed a class and I always read the chapter before the class and I made sure to do every single homework assignment.

Some of you might be thinking a few things. One, you might be thinking, *You must be extremely smart because I do those things, but I don't see success.* Or two, you might be thinking, *You aren't taking hard classes as a theology major!* And you might be a nursing major, engineering or some major with intense classes.

I actually remember when I had finished the semester with all As, a girl in the nursing program said to me, "That's because you are taking easy classes! Try taking a class like Anatomy and Physiology (A&P) or one of these nursing classes." There they go again, people trying to ruin our excitement. But what took place later that week changed a lot for me, and answers some of those questions that you might have.

I was sitting down with my advisor going over the classes that I had to take for next semester. He mentioned to me that I had to take another science class and the only thing that was available for next semester was Anatomy & Physiology II. So he said, "We will have to just wait for next year." In that moment, I cut him off and said, "Sign me up!" He looked at me, puzzled, and said, "Are you sure? This is a hard class, and you will also have Greek II and this isn't A&P I, this is A&P II." I was confident I wanted to take the class! Students were allowed to take A&P II without taking A&P I because the first class dealt with anatomy and the second class with the physiology. They had very little overlap, which makes it hard but not impossible. He told me to talk with the professor before making my decision.

I remember walking up to Dr. Mchenry's office for the first time and asking him what he thought about me taking his class. He told me that people have done it before and it works out well, but I would have to put my best foot forward—finally someone not ruining the excitement. I asked him the golden question, "What do I have to do in order to succeed?" Same answer: read the book before class, don't skip class, and do the labs—in this case there wasn't any homework, it was just labs.

The first day of class was crazy. Just so you get a little background, I knew nothing about A&P. I didn't even know what the letters stood for. I didn't know what was in my body at all. I knew I had a heart, a stomach, lungs and some intestines. It was crazy that I was even taking this class, now that I think of it. But during that first day we went over the syllabus and I never will forget how the class ended. He asked the question, "How does the heart work?" The only thing that came to my mind was, "God?" But everyone started yelling out things like "The heart has chambers," "Valves," and "Muscles." And I was so confused thinking to myself, "What? A heart has all that?"

I knew that I had to take it up a notch. So I carried around a notebook in the class, and as the professor did the lecture anytime a question popped up in my mind I would write it down. After class I would find the professor and ask him the questions, or the teacher's assistant. Sometimes the questions got answered as we continued the lecture. Some days I had five questions and other days it was like twenty-five questions. The awesome thing is, when tests came they were easy. That's because all of the questions I had throughout the class were getting answered. I ended up finishing the class that semester with an A—and a slight desire to go into the medical field, which I did not do.

Something that I realized I was doing and something I still use today is something that I call "filling the gaps." When we sit in a class and we are learning something— or when we are learning from someone online or just on our own—there are questions that naturally pop up. And for some reason the older we get the less we want to ask questions, because we feel like we should know or we feel dumb or embarrassed asking the question. Everyone knows that kids are amazing learners, and I wonder if the reason they are amazing learners is because they aren't afraid to ask questions. You hear them ask all the time, "Why?" They ask their parents, teachers, older siblings—at times it's annoying, but it helps them learn of the world around them. But then after a while we just assume we now know everything because we are grown up and we stop asking that question.

When we learn, it's like stacking blocks on top of each other. The first row is like the foundation of the topic. Once you understand the basics, you can move on to the next level and that helps you get to the next level. And eventually you become an expert over time. It is like learning how to add numbers together, if you haven't understood how to add single digits, are you going to understand how to add double digits? No, of course not. But if you have that solid foundation of adding single digits, double digits won't be difficult. As a matter of fact, as you learn, it's easier to understand because you are familiar with the basics of adding single digits.

But what happens when you don't have that sure foundation? Let me put it this way. When you are sitting in the class and the teacher says something you don't understand, what happens then next time the teacher talks about that topic? You won't understand it completely. This is where we begin to have questions in our mind like, "What?" or even statements like, "I have no clue what she is talking about." Instead of being discouraged because you don't understand, write down what you don't understand and ask the question after class.

The thing that is awesome about writing down questions is that it helps you keep up with everything that is happening in the class. It allows you to have that good foundation with your blocks so you can be ready for the next level. What happens when you don't understand something? Keep asking questions until it makes sense. Literally do not stop until it makes sense to you, especially if you will be building on it more down the road in your class. There were some days I would be in Dr. Mchenry's office for two hours answering questions. I would talk to tutors, I would talk to anyone that understood it, until it was answered and I could repeat it back to them. Don't be satisfied with confusion! But ask questions. That can be the greatest skill any learner can learn.

What I love about asking questions is it does something else for us. It brings up our curiosity for the subject. Why is that important? Because it will make us genuinely interested in the topic. It brings us an appreciation for the topic and helps us to be interested in what we are learning. The more we understand how something works, the more we will have a passion for that thing. Think about anything that you are passionate about. You are probably passionate about it because you know a lot about it. You know how it works on a simple level and you know how it works on a complicated level. Asking questions can get you to the point where you have no idea about a subject and a few months later you want to change your major—talking about myself, I wanted to change my major but I didn't end up doing it.

This is how I made it through Greek and how I also made it through A&P II. It wasn't easy. You have to put in the work, but when you put in the work early, as you go up in blocks it will get easier. Greek II for me was easy, because I had such an amazing foundation in Greek I. Towards the end of A&P II, I was not nervous about the final exam, because I had a great foundation. This can apply to anything that you are learning, in class or outside of class. Really, if you want to get something down, ask questions. Build that foundation with all the questions you have and you will be able to make it through anything!

How to begin building a foundation of questions

1. Begin carrying a notebook to class for each subject. *(As is fitting for the class.)*

2. Every time the teacher says something that you don't understand, write it down in the notebook in the form of a question. *(What does _____ have to do with _____?)*

3. Each day sometime after class, find the teacher or the teacher's assistant and ask them all the questions in your notebook until you are **fully** satisfied that you understand.

4

Best Seat in the House

What seat would you take, if you were offered a seat at a concert where your favorite band or artist was going to perform? Or what about at a sporting event for your favorite team? Would you select the seats that are all the way up in the nosebleeds? Or would you aim to get a seat all the way up front with no one in front of you? Or would it not matter where you sat, so you would just tell the person, "Get me a seat wherever!"

Well, if you are anything like me, you would be going for the seats all the way in the front. One of the first times I went to a professional musical performance, I sat all the way in the front row. I remember watching all the different people playing on their instruments and I even have vivid pictures in my mind of what the person was wearing and what they were playing, and even some facial expressions. It was a super-special night because it felt almost like they were playing just for me.

Whether people like to admit it or not, there is power in sitting in the front seat—that why we like sitting there for things that interest us. There is power sitting in the front seat that will help you in many aspects of life. I know reading this, you may be like *Really? Sitting in the front could help me?* But I am convinced that the closer you sit to the front of the class, the easier you make the class. When I began taking anatomy and physiology, I knew that I was going to have to sit in the front because I wanted to be focused and I wanted to hear everything the teacher had to say.

I didn't realize the importance of sitting in the front seat until one day, I decided to sit with a friend in class, and we walked all the way to the back of the class and sat down. First let me just mention that I had no idea there were that many people in the class—at least it looked like more from the back. It looked like the number was over one hundred. I could see the entire class, which didn't do a lot of good for me, for several reasons.

The first is how distracting the back seat can be. Let's be honest with ourselves, when we are sitting and we have one hundred people in front of us, any time something happens on your left side, what happens? You look. What about the right side? You look. What about right in front of you? You look. You can see the person who isn't paying attention, and that probably distracts you or makes you frustrated. You see that person playing games on their laptop and it throws you off. Sitting in the back can be very distracting, where if we were sitting in the front we wouldn't have those distractions. There would be nothing in the front, just the teacher.

The second reason to avoid sitting in the back is that you don't feel as comfortable raising your hand and asking a question if you end up getting lost. There is something that is intimidating, especially if you are not extroverted, when it comes to having attention on you. When you are sitting in the back and you raise your hand to ask a question, as soon as you talk the whole class is turned around looking at you. So what ends up happening? Because in reality, no one wants to attract all that attention. What ends up happening instead is that we make some sly comment to the person sitting next to us, like, "I have no idea what the professor is talking about."

When I sat with my friend in the back of the class, I remember thinking to myself how awkward it was to just raise my hand and ask a question. I remember one time specifically, forcing myself to ask a question and when everyone turned around, it felt weird with everyone just staring at me. I am an extrovert—I like attention—but even that felt a little weird. I don't recall ever asking a question the rest of that class period, but I knew that was going to be the last time I sat all the way in the back.

The third reason to sit up front is—and I know I sound like a teacher's pet, but it's not what it sounds like—because it felt as though the teacher was just teaching me. The reason we are willing to sit in the front for all these other things we love in life, whether it's theatre, a concert, or a sporting event, is because it gives us this feeling that no one else is in the room. It helps us to lock in and focus on the moment. The reason we sit in the back of the class at school is because we don't care too much about what the teacher has to say, or maybe even the subject. But that's just the thing, sitting in the front of class helps to ignite a level of that excitement, because it feels as though the teacher is not just trying to teach the class something, but that the teacher is trying to teach *you* something.

Sitting in the front of class, all I saw was my professor and the whiteboard. When I sat in the back, I could see the whole class, nearly every student. It no longer felt as though it was me and the teacher, but rather the teacher, the class, and I happened to be part of the class.

There is a Bible verse in Romans 12:1 that tells us, "Let us lay aside every weight and the sin which so easily ensnares us, and let us run with endurance the race set before us." This is in relation to sin, but the principle still stands. In college, we are running a race. The race to graduation. If you can't see down that road yet, it could be the race to the end of the semester. You might be almost there, or you might have a long way to go. Either way, when you are running this race, don't you want the race to be easier? Why would we make the race to graduation harder on ourselves? When we sit in the back of the class, I am convinced that we make it harder on ourselves.

I had one friend who began the semester sitting in the front together with me. We both were doing really well in the class. I would almost say that we had one of the highest grades. As the semester continued, I saw him move closer and closer to the back. And later in the semester, I asked him how he was doing in the class and he said, "Not too good, I feel like I am barely making it." I know there is a reality of the temptation to sit with your friends in class or even a significant other. But don't feel like you have to give up the best seat in the house for it, especially if you are in a class that you really want to succeed in.

Here are some other ways sitting in the front helped. It helped me stay off my phone. You know the temptation is real, and when you have the teacher right in front of you, you are not as tempted to go on your phone. It also helps with not sleeping as much in class—though my roommate in college found ways to still do that, so don't feel bad if you do. It also helped the teacher know that I am serious about the class.

I challenge you to try it out. The next time you are in class, just try sitting in the front of the class first and then switch to the back and you will see for yourself. Sitting in the front has its benefits and makes running this race a lot smoother. After sitting in the front of the class for three years at Southwestern Adventist University, I can testify that this works! The front seat is truly the best seat in the house.

Best seat in the house

1. Try sitting in the front of a class for two months of one semester and see the difference that it makes in your grades and retention of material.

5

Get Involved!

For some people coming into college, you may have no idea at all what you want to do, or even how you are going to make genuine friendships that will last. Well, there is a way that you can actually do both. I know, crazy! Just follow me.

When I first stepped foot on the campus of SWAU, I knew that I wanted either a job on campus, a volunteer position or to be part of a club. I had this theory that those who are involved with some form of work get better grades. One way that getting involved with some form of work will help you is in the area of getting things done.

This was a theory that I had run across working as a dean at Great Lakes Adventist Academy. Think about it this way, people who have less time tend to procrastinate less. And people who have more time tend to procrastinate the most! It's that procrastinating voice inside of your head that tells you over and over again, "I have time" that makes you procrastinate.

We all, at some point, have run across that person on campus—and if you are not a college student yet, you will see this person—who seems to have time to hang out all day and they seem to not have a packed schedule, or sometimes no schedule at all. Then you get the news that they are not doing so well at the school. On the other hand you have someone with a packed schedule, who seems to not be able to fit in anything. They are the people who are doing better in classes. The reason that is the case is because they value the time that they have, because it is limited. People who get involved tend to get better grades!

Involvement also helps with creating meaningful friendships. There are other places where you make friends, aside from class. You never thought that's how you make good, long-lasting friends, did you? How are friends made? Have you ever thought about that? Think about it this way, you make friends based on your geographic location, based on proximity. the places that you are forced to be at. places like your room—your roommate if they are cool. Classes—if you work on projects or connect with people to study. Work, volunteer and clubs! Involvement! Think about your closest friends. Where did you meet them? At work? At school? In your neighborhood? Sports? At church? It is all based on location.

One time walking on campus, I remember seeing a guy that I always kind of thought was a cool guy, but if someone asked me where I would put him on the scales for being a ladies' man, I wouldn't have given him anything over a 5, that's for sure. One day, I remember walking on campus with a friend and we looked over and we saw him with a girl that we both classified as gorgeous. We literally said to ourselves, how did a guy like that get a girl like that! You might have some people that come to your mind when you think of our situation. It's crazy, isn't it?

We ended up brushing it off, and we continued forward with life. And one day I saw him and the same girl in the cafeteria; it turns out that they worked together in the cafe! That is the power of proximity! If you want to build relationships—not just romantically, we will get to that in a later chapter—then find ways to get involved on campus! Some my closest friends came from the jobs that I had when I was on the campus. You will be surprised by how much of an impact it will have in your life at college.

There are some realities that you might encounter when you begin searching for ways to get involved. You might encounter the reality that there are no jobs on your campus, and it might feel impossible to find a job in your college town area. Well, I have a key: work as a volunteer. No one really likes the idea of volunteering, but the truth is volunteer work gets you in the door many more times than you can imagine compared to paid work.

When I was in college I worked in what is called the Spiritual Life and Development office. And working there, I came to realize that as an office we needed volunteers. Just like at every institution, volunteers make the wheels turn. There may be days when they aren't as needed, but at some point or another, they will be needed. The best part is, when it came to hiring for the next semester, because we were always hiring someone new, we always looked at our volunteers first, before looking to people that just put in a resume. Volunteer work still does the job of putting you around people on a consistent basis, which is exactly what you need to develop those friendships.

Another area where being involved helps is figuring out what you want to do with your future. Coming into college, there is always that group of people who say they have no idea what they want to do, either with their major or for a career—and I was that person, by the way. What ends up happening is they start to work their way through college doing the bare minimum in hopes that one day, the career they want is just going to hit them over the head and be like, "Here I am!" But let's be honest with ourselves, does that ever happen? No, not necessarily. How is it that there are people who know exactly what they want to do at age 12, and then you have people who are going for their master's degree and they are still not sure?

I am convinced that the problem is they have not been involved enough. They haven't been involved in enough volunteer work and they haven't been involved in that many jobs. They haven't been involved in club— either starting or being a part of one. They haven't been involved in anything that would have been able to ignite in them that passion. Are you wanting to find passion? Get involved in something! Get involved in everything. If you have no idea, do something that is more temporary like volunteer work or attending a club event. If you know what you want to do, go for something more serious like a job or sign up to be a member of a club.

At the university that I attended, we had something that was called Enactus; you may have it at your school as well. This was a business club that was on campus that literally anyone could be a part of, no matter what your major was.

I remember there was a girl who joined this club, and she was one of the shyest girls I feel as though I ever met, but over time, the club gave her confidence to do things that were out of her comfort zone! It wasn't over the course of a semester but rather over the course of some years. But that is the power of getting involved. Not only did that help her come out of her shell, but she ended up finding a passion in business she didn't know existed in her.

I know there is a temptation to sit down in your room. Trust me, I know that feeling of being in your dorm room thinking to yourself, "Why am I here?" And the feeling of calling someone back home, just so that you don't have to feel like you're alone. I also know the temptation to hang out with friends and just coast your way through college. But when you step on a college campus, there is so much for you to be a part of. There are so many clubs. There are so many job opportunities. There are so many places to do volunteer work. When you just take time to observe it and jump into it, you will be surprised at what will come from being involved.

Ways to get involved

1. Volunteering in an area of interest is a great way to start. It is less permanent and can give you a taste of what you would get into if you made a deeper commitment. *(If you aren't sure where to begin, ask a friend or a family member or a faculty/staff member.)*

2. Get a job on campus. Make a list of ten different jobs that you would not mind doing on campus, and begin working through that list, putting in job applications and following up on them. *(On-campus jobs love it when you come in person so they can put a face to the application.)*

3. Join a club. Find a club on campus that you relate most with and join it. *(If there is no club on campus that interests you, join a club through a friend on campus or a faculty/staff member that you respect.)*

4. Join an extracurricular activity. This would be more based on the abilities that you have. Try out for a sports team, join an orchestra or a band, join the choir, join the gymnastics team. *(Even if*

you don't make it one year, that doesn't mean you can't practice/train for the chance to do it the next.)

5. Attend events on campus. We may think that this is obvious, but you will be surprised how many students don't attend events that are made available to them.

6

Me? President?

When I first arrived on the campus of Southwestern Adventist University, I knew absolutely nobody. You might be experiencing something like that, or maybe you have already experienced something like that. Being on the campus was intimidating, but I knew that I wanted to succeed, especially in the realm of socializing. So, I implemented the steps I have mentioned so far in this book.

I got a job in the Spiritual Life and Development office. I got a job doing custodial work, which, I would like to mention, was my favorite job. Where else can you listen to music and work at the same time? Make phone calls and work at the same time? That was my job. And many times, it was therapeutic. I was a part of a small group called Daily Life House, or Light House—we still argue about the name today. I played the tuba back in high school and so I joined the orchestra. And towards the end of the semester I ended up doing a little volunteer work in the cafeteria as well. The cook was in need of some help when it came to the pots and pans, and since I had done that in high school, I thought I could be of assistance.

As you can see, my schedule was pretty booked up! But what was really cool was how I was making friends in so many different locations. Over time I got more and more comfortable on the campus because I had my finger dipped in a lot of areas. Again, for some people doing as much as I did might be overwhelming, but I would advise taking it step by step.

The next semester, the student government had their elections taking place but for me it was the furthest thing from my mind. I literally was not even fully aware that elections were coming up. One morning I woke up and I didn't even realize that it was the last day to put in your request for a position. I was walking through the administration building, as I normally do, and I ran across a friend who stopped me and said, "Samson! You have to run for president!" I wanted to laugh because the idea just sounded ridiculous. I didn't even know what the position consisted of, so why would I do that? I apologized to my friend and kept going.

About five minutes later I went in to meet with a faculty member and I ran across another friend. This guy was what some of us may call a troll. He loved instigating, he loved playing with people and picking their brains, and he for sure loved controversy. He said to me, in a slightly sarcastic voice, "Samson, you should run for president. You would make a good president." I knew immediately that he was just messing with me, so I just laughed it off and continued with my day.

I went into the cafeteria and grabbed some food. While I was there, I ran into a good friend of mine. As we were just chatting about our day, she said to me, "Samson, you should do student government." I thought to myself, "Oh no, not this again." She continued, "I really feel like you would make a good president." In that moment, everything seemed to slow down. I thought to myself, "What if God is trying to tell me something?" I can ignore one or two comments, but three felt like there might be something there.

I decided to put in the application to run for office. I didn't really tell a lot of people that I did it, because I wanted to pray over the weekend and think about it. As the weekend was coming to a close, the thought that I had was, "Let me ask my mom. Whatever she says, I will go with." My momma is wise like that. I told her the situation and she responded with, "Don't go for the position, you are busy as is and no need to kill yourself." As relaxed as can be, my response was, "You're right, Mom, I am going to remove my name on Monday." Then she interrupted me with, "Wait, if you already put your name in, just leave it and let God decide for you. I thought you hadn't put it in yet." My heart dropped into my stomach. I just did not expect her to switch her answer that quickly. The situation got a lot more real.

The time came closer and closer. Word started to spread that I was running for president. This random kid from Michigan, who does not know anyone. When it came time for the speeches, I didn't want to just come up with a speech of all the things that I wanted to do, because I didn't even really know what I could do. I didn't want to make empty promises, so instead I shared, "I don't know what I am doing." Imagine that for a prospective president's speech. But I continued, "I have been in these situations before, and I have done my best and God blessed."

A lot of people came up to me, asking why I would make a speech about how "I don't know what I am doing" if I am running for this position. It was one of those moments when I just accepted the fact that I might not get this position. And I was cool with it. When it came time for the announcements about who won, I remember sitting in the cafeteria when someone said, "Samson! You got it!" I was super puzzled. "I did?" How does a kid out of nowhere who doesn't know anybody win a student government position in less than a year? That question plagued my mind.

I remember driving in the car with a friend of mine and I was just telling them how confused I was that I won. She said, "I didn't really doubt it." When I asked her why, I will never forget her response. She said,

"Because you make people feel comfortable and you have a lot of friends in a lot of different groups."

I guess it turns out that being involved and seeking to make people comfortable has its advantages. I would in no way say that if you follow this path you will be student government president at your university. What I am saying is that it works. All you have to do is apply it. You will be amazed by the impact that you can make on your college or university in the span of a few days, weeks, months or years.

It's like the story in the Bible, when God speaks to Joshua in Joshua 1:3 and He says, "Wherever land your foot trends on, I have given it to you." Everywhere that Joshua puts his foot down, it belongs to him. How many places have we not received because we are afraid to put our foot down? Or because we are nervous to put our foot down? I believe that everyone has the potential to do something awesome on their campus, you just have to be willing to move.

When we walk onto a college campus, we have no idea what awaits us. There are opportunities after opportunities that are just waiting for us. Some of those opportunities are hiding behind the small things that we can do today. I never imagined that being involved and seeking to make others comfortable could land me in the places that I have gone. But the same is true for you. You will be more than surprised at what can get worked out for you, if you take those little steps of faith. You will never guess where you will end up.

Leap of faith

1. What is something that you have been wanting to do, but you have been afraid or nervous about trying it? Whether it is being uncomfortable for others to be comfortable, or getting involved with something on the campus, try doing something and just see what happens.

7

Did I Mention Mentors?

When I jumped into the presidency of my college's student government, I had absolutely no idea what I was doing. I felt as though, at the time, winning the election was one of the scariest things that had happened to me. But just as it was starting to sink in that this was the path that I was going on now, I knew that I could not do it alone.

Immediately, after I had won the election. I began going from department to department and from office to office getting to know the staff and faculty. I went almost to every single office. The line I would say in every situation was the same, "Hi, my name is Samson and I just got elected as student government president and I just wanted to know what you do in your office/position." I was a lost little confused boy, looking for some type of direction. But what I didn't notice was that I was actually building relationships with many of the staff members on campus. There were staff and faculty that have told me they never really knew who the student government presidents were because they never interacted with them.

As the year began to progress, these were the same people who helped me through every part of my presidency. People tell me all the time, even today, how amazing our team was, but the reality that they don't know about was that we had people in our corner who were mentoring us and giving us wisdom to make decisions.

You might be thinking to yourself, *Wait a second, I can't just go into every department and say I am the president.* And that may be true, but something that you can do is find ways to surround yourself with people in your department and other departments where you have interests. You can surround yourself with people that you see are willing to invest in you. This isn't saying that you have to be a teacher's pet and "suck up" to a teacher. This is saying that you cannot do what you are trying to do in life alone; you need people surrounding you giving you the advice you need to succeed. This is true whether those are things that you are trying to do in college or later in life after college.

Going through college, I had several mentors who helped me when it came to making decisions about what to major in, about jobs after school, and even regarding my love life. And guess what? They are still in my life today after graduating giving me advice in the work field and life.

College and university is one of the best places to find mentors. Where else can you go to find a wide variety of people from different backgrounds who are all educated in some way, and who have connections with people in different areas in the work field? Some may be educated in the practical things of life, and some may be educated when it come to the more philosophical things. Both are good types of education, and both are needed. The thing that keeps us from finding mentors is that we think people are too busy for us. In reality, older people—especially staff and faculty who work at the college level—are constantly looking to invest in people.

I remember thinking to myself, I really don't want to bother the president of the university. I had ideas and thoughts that I wanted to bring up to him. Also, I wanted to develop a relationship between the student government and the administration. But I told myself I'd just do one meeting and then I wouldn't have to do another. After sitting down with the president for twenty minutes, just getting to know each other and talking about our thoughts on the school, we ended up setting aside time every two months or so to catch up. Now, if the president of the university had time for me, I can guarantee that there are many others—staff members, faculty—that would take the time to invest in you.

As I was going from office to office and from department to department. I walked into the room of the vice president of the school, Amy Rosenthal. I loved one of the things that she mentioned to me before I left her office. She said, "I know you may not feel like you know what you are doing, but going into the offices and getting to know everyone is wise." And this is where she got me: "Because knowledge is power. The more you know, and the more people you know, will help you succeed."

Think about it. You have staff and faculty, who have had decades of experiences, some in the field that you want to go into when you graduate. You have an opportunity to build relationships, to have mentors who can help you with decisions now, and decisions in the future. Imagine just three mentors who have thirty years of experience each. That would be ninety years of experience that you get to have going throughout life, specifically, in the field that you are in—and even if it's not in your field, that still is very valuable.

You might be thinking to yourself, *But of course people invested in you. If I were the student government president they would invest in me too.* But just so you know, even before I became the student government president, people were looking to invest in me, because that is the reality of staff and faculty. From professors to faculty, there are people who long to invest in someone who is willing to take the time to invest in themselves.

I remember coming on to the campus the first time. I would ask staff and faculty, "What would you recommend I get involved with?" "What advice do you have for succeeding here as a student?" "How long have you worked here? And what is your advice to having a good college experience here?" I would start off with these types of questions just to build a simple relationship with the staff and faculty members. I would eventually move to questions like, "How do you feel people can be prepared for life after graduation?" "If you could start over and go back to college what would you do differently now?" These questions started to become more personal.

If you don't know who to start with I would recommend starting with the staff that you remember most from registration day. There were people that stuck out to you and that happened for a reason. After, I would go next to the faculty that are in the department where you have your major. Connect with them and talk about careers. Last, I would go to the staff and faculty that are in charge of the departments that you have interest in. Get to know them. I know that it can feel intimidating, but when you remember that those on the campus want to invest in you more than you want to be invested in, it will help you have more confidence.

I ask you the question, who do you know? Who can you know? Do you have mentors? People that you can go to for questions about school? Questions about ideas that you have? Questions about life in general? If you are willing to sit down and find some mentors, I can assure you that you will be able to have more wisdom than you can imagine. It reminds me of the verse in the Bible that tells us, "There is wisdom in the counsel of many." When you have the right people in your corner, you will have everything that you need to succeed in college and even after.

Ways to find mentors

1. After the first few weeks of school, ask yourself who are some staff members or professors you relate to or connect with the most? You can make a list of five or six people.

2. Ask them questions. Questions about their class, questions about how to succeed at the school. When it comes to staff members, ask them, "What is the secret to surviving at this school?" When it comes to professors, ask them "What is the secret to getting an A in your class?" Ask them what they love most about the school. Starting off, just ask very light questions.

3. Ask them deeper questions. Over time (a month or two of running into them), ask them deeper questions, dealing with your future and what they would do in your shoes. That is when they transition from being a faculty/staff member to being a mentor.

4. Ask them to be your mentor. If someone on campus has been investing in you (taking the time to answer questions or thoughts you have

while sharing their own experience), they would be more than willing to become your mentor.

8

Experiment! Experiment! Experiment!

Attending college and university doesn't only have benefits when it comes to social interactions and building a network. It also works wonders when it comes to your professional growth and your innovation and creativity development. When we talked about getting involved, that was all about utilizing what already exists on the campus in order to find your passion and to make friends. But now we are entering experimenting, which is you bringing value to the campus that you attend.

When I became the student government president, it opened up to me wonders as to what could happen on a campus. It showed me how anything is possible, whatever project that you want to do on a campus can get done. One of the things that I really wanted to implement was a service day for the entire campus. And after going back and forth with the administration, because the details were very important, it ended up eventually being approved. Now the school has a service day that they do every year.

I know you might be thinking, *How on earth am I going to put something together like a service day for the campus?* That's not the point of the story. The point is, what do you want to do? Literally stop and ask yourself the question. What do you want to do in life? This can be related to your major or just something you think would be fun on the side. What is stopping you from doing it? Doing the service day was nowhere in the student government job description. It was just something that I wanted to do. I came to realize after that experience, that if there is anything I ever want to do, college is the best place to do it! The same thing is true for you. If there is any project you want to embark on, college is the best place to do it!

Think about it this way. When you come in as a freshman, you have four years (or maybe two at community college) to try or implement anything that you want. This can be a business idea, this can be a project to start at the school, or it can be you building your experience level in your field by experimenting on the campus. There are so many people on the campus who are at your fingertips, whether it's students in the classroom, in the library and all over campus, or even faculty and staff that are willing to help you with the ideas that you have!

My roommate in college is a perfect example of this. He is an art major. And you might be thinking there isn't much that an art major can do in college except take the classes that they might need to take and then graduate and pray for a job. A lot of people even hold the assumption that when they graduate, art majors may not even get a job. But something cool my roommate did was he opened his own gallery on the campus. Mind you, he worked with a teacher on campus and she helped, but a lot of what was going on was dependent on him. He did the art pieces, found a venue on campus, did the advertising and he ended up selling some of those pieces for a very good price.

What is stopping us from doing the same thing? Maybe not an art gallery, but what else can you do? We might be thinking to ourselves, *What if I ask a teacher for help and I get rejected? Or what if they think it's a bad idea?* I am here to tell you to find someone who believes and if it's a bad idea they will help you to fix it.

The first time I brought up the idea of a service day for the entire campus, the administration thought that it was a difficult thing to pull off. They told me why it wouldn't work and I went back to my room, changed up some stuff and went back to them and asked again. They told me some more things that needed fixing and I went back to my room, changed some of the details and I came back again. And again. and again. Until one day they were like, "You know, this just might work." I also had to find other faculty that believed in it—and they exist, trust me. Even if you don't find them, you can still have an idea and run with it, because you are on a college campus and there are so many people around you.

During my last year at Southwestern Adventist University, I became really close to two guys, Josh Ramirez and Eliab Quinones, who were also theology majors. And coming to the last two weeks of school, we had the idea to do a sermon series on the problems that students faced when it came to a relationship with Jesus. This wasn't something that was approved through the school necessarily, just something that we decided to do. Students had all kinds of small groups on campus so this was a bigger version of that. We rented out a space and we made it happen. We ended up having a full house show up and it lasted for a week. The university ended up helping us out with the cost, because they saw the impact it was making. Not only that, but after we graduated, they invited us to come back and do that same series for the whole campus.

You will never know what your experiments will do for you or for the campus. We were theology majors, so we went the route of a sermon series. But what business idea do you have? What are you passionate about that you want to try to do? Are you into communications? Practice doing advertising for a club or a department. Are you into business? Start a business on campus. Are you into English? Maybe start an editing business or even write short novels. Are you into languages? Start something along the lines of translating. Are you into the arts? Set up an art gallery. You have hundreds and thousands of people to test your products or ideas on, so take advantage of it.

I wouldn't be your friend if I didn't tell you the obvious flip side to experimenting and trying things. And that is the reality that you might fail—some say that you will fail when you try things for the first time. But failure is not bad. Sometimes when you fail at something it is just that you are learning how *not* to do something. Failure is actually very, very valuable.

When I was in my last year at Southwestern, another project that I wanted to try was something to help with our health on campus. Our campus was highly focused on health, and I wanted to do something to get everyone excited about health. So I did a challenge for three months where everyone got a chance to document a checklist of healthy things to do every day. In the end we would tally up the score and whatever range you ended up in, that would be the prize you won. Well, guess how many people got involved in it? It was worse than whatever number you just imagined in your head. There were three participants, including me. I thank the other two that were a part of it..

I learned so much from doing that challenge for the campus. You can say the first thing I learned was how not to do it. But that is just as important as learning how to do it, because it is paving the way to helping you get there next time. There are tons of things that I would change if I had the opportunity to do it again. Some of you might be thinking to yourselves, *But you graduated and that is it! You won't be able to do it again.* But that is just the thing. Whatever you learn in college, whatever you experiment with in college, you take the experience with you into the world. Think about that.

No one will ever take away the fact that I know how to organize a service day for a large group of people in a community. No one will ever take away from my roommate that he knows how to put on an art gallery at any time he wants. No one will ever take away from my friends and me that we know how to organize a sermon series on a campus—and really anywhere. No one will ever take away from me that I know how to organize a health challenge—or even how not to do it. Whether it is an experience that went well or one that did not go so well, you still have that experience. And something really cool is I get to do this health challenge for the church where I am a pastor. Second chance! I could be anywhere with people who want to enhance their health and say, "I did a health challenge in college."

And get this. this is my favorite part. When it comes to college campuses, whenever you want to do some type of project or try something out, failing in college is a lot easier than failing in the world outside of college. College is a safe place. Look at it this way. In college, for a lot of the ideas that you have, departments exist to help push those ideas. If not the department, maybe there are clubs that have budgets for ideas just like what you are thinking. There are budgets that are all over the campus. And some of those budgets don't get rolled over to the next year, meaning they want to spend it, because it will be gone by the end of the year anyway. Guess what? If the service day had failed, I would not have been out anything financially. When I failed with the health challenge, I was not out a single dollar. But imagine if it had been outside of college? I probably would have been out a lot more.

Whatever project that you want to experiment with, you can connect with people on campus and they will be more than excited to help you get it done. The failures you have in college don't follow you on a resume; rather, they help build it since that is experience for you. But sadly, the world outside of college doesn't get too excited about failure. Make sure to embrace the beauty of a college campus being a safe place for you to experiment.

It's not just that, but you are in the network of hundreds and thousands (and sometimes tens of thousands) of people. That means you get to test and try your experiments on them before you go out into the world—where finding those people will be harder. We may say that we can find those people on social media, but the reality is building that experience in person is better than trying to build it online. What I love about experimenting on campuses is, imagine if you fail at something in college? The awesome thing is you will have a new group coming in the next year (freshmen), and then a new group coming in the year after that. You will literally have an endless group of people coming every year, giving you time to work on different projects or experiments you want to try and even grow in what you've already done before.

You have no idea what you are capable of accomplishing at your college or university. If you are willing to experiment, if you are willing to do something you have never done before, you will find out more quickly than you know what is really inside you. What ideas do you have? What do you want to embark on? Is there anything that you want to try? What is stopping you from going and making it happen? Are you waiting until after you graduate? Then you might end up waiting longer than that. Start experimenting today and you will be surprised by how things turn out!

Ways to experiment on your campus

1. What is your major in college? What are some things that you can do on the campus that are in relation to your major? *(If you get stuck, ask a mentor for advice.)*

2. What are some passions that you have? (Art, photography, sports, etc.) Literally, it can be anything. What are ways you can incorporate those ideas on your campus? *(Getting inspiration from what other people have done on their campus is a great place to start. YouTube and Google are your friends.)*

3. Ask yourself what ideas you saw someone implement before that you thought were really cool (online or stories you heard from another campus). Is there a way you could add your special touch to it? Try replicating it with your special touch.

4. What do you feel like your campus is missing? What is something you feel students could benefit from if it were on your campus? Try

implementing the missing piece on a small scale and see how it kicks off.

5. Don't be afraid to just try something small or go big. Just do it! Get the people that you need around you to make it happen and just do it. And you will be surprised by how much you learn and grow from each experiment's success or failure. *(But it is always a success in the end if you learn from it.)*

9

Goodbye, Social Media!

Now, this is not a chapter about how you need to get rid of your social media or that you need to get rid of your smartphone. Let's be honest, we are in college; we need those devices. Remember, this book is about getting the most out of college. And one area that is really important to the college experience is in the area of our smartphones and social media. Everyone has one! Literally.

Towards the end of my time at Southwestern, I decided that I wanted to get signed up for counseling— and that was not something I thought I would ever do in my life, don't worry, I will share more about this experience in a later chapter. But one of the things that came out of that experience was my use of social media.

I didn't know how much it was affecting me, but I came to understand that I needed to do something about it. Something crazy—because let's face it, if you got to this point in the book, you know I have a little bit of crazy in me.

Now if you are from Texas or you have been in Texas anytime in the month of August or September, you might be familiar with the State Fair of Texas. With it being my last year at Southwestern, I knew that I had to attend—otherwise I might never attend the fair. So lucky for me, I had two really good friends who I knew would take me there, and I was so thankful for it. Now, whoever has been to the State Fair knows about the crazy traffic and the intense amount of people. We ended up sitting in the car waiting for the traffic, for what felt like hours.

Finally, we got to the fair and we were enjoying ourselves—the fair was an amazing experience. After arriving,, there was the iconic picture that everyone must take in-front of the Big Tex statue. Now I was pretty cool with this, as it was something that was "iconic." But I remember it coming to a point where we ran everywhere trying to get pictures of all the iconic things at the fair—maybe I shouldn't have gone with girls, not sure what the answer is there. Even though it was a good time at the fair, something that really crossed my mind was how we missed so many things at the fair because we were trying to get those iconic pictures, in order to post on social media. We were so focused on documenting the experience that we forgot to actually *have* the experience.

Everyone wants their life to look like the most interesting life. We want to make it look like we do fun or amazing things. We want to show the world that we have it together. Don't get me wrong, it's cool to see what your friends are up to, and it's cool to update your friends, but what about the desperation to want to show them everything? What about the desperation to let everyone know you are on the trend as well? What about examining the lives of others to the point where you want what they have? This is where the danger comes. Because something happens on the dark side. We end up losing our physical life and replacing it with a virtual life. If we can say "Go on my profile," then we don't have to be good in person. And that superficial experience transfers, not just for ourselves but also to our friendships. No "like" on social media can beat a compliment in real life. Examining someone's post on social media will never beat a conversation and understanding how they got to where they are at.

Going into my last year of college, I began to spend way too much time on my social media. I began to realize that I was beginning to wish I had more. More friends, more fun, more money, more romance, etc. This may not be the case for everyone, but if we are being honest, we have all fallen down the path at least once where we saw someone's social media page and "wished" for whatever they were showing us. What do we do with those feelings? I remember one time, I was scrolling on social media and I saw a group of my friends all at a location enjoying themselves and literally thought to myself, "Wow, they really don't miss me or even think to invite me." You might have felt that feeling before, some call it FOMO (fear of missing out).

Going into the year 2019, I decided to get rid of my social media for the entire year. Now this is not what

I am going to recommend to you—though I think everyone should get rid of their social media for a year at least once. But rather, what I am going to share is the lessons that I have learned and how I believe taking a break from social media helped me go through my last semester in college.

When I decided to eliminate social media for a year, I counted the cost of what I was going to be missing out on sharing. It was going to be the year I graduated from college, the year I was going to start working at my first church as a pastor, the year when I was going to want to show the social media world the most. But I knew that getting rid of social media was going to be a greatest experience for me.

The first lesson that I learned was you begin to be more intentional. When it comes to the funny stuff that you run across in life, we all know what to do. We take out our phones and we record the situation. Not just for the benefit of our own lives to look back to, but rather we do it to post on social media so we can get people to see that funny stuff happens in our life or on some platforms so it goes viral—unless you have another reason to post it? But when you don't have social media, I noticed it fell into two categories. Either I sent it to a friend because I knew they would find it funny or I would just sit in that moment and enjoy it—if it is really funny I will record It and go back to it later in life as well. But what was cool about it is that the moment was very personal to me, not just something to post to the world. It was amazing because I could message a friend and they would laugh at it, and many times start conversations. It was personal.

Another lesson that I learned was that it helped me to be more in the moment. I heard a saying once that, "A person that is a good texter is horrible company in person, and the person that is the greatest company in person is the worst texter." Not sure how true it is, but the principle sure speaks volumes. When I got off social media, I began to see how we can be hanging out with a group of people and be so far from everyone at the same time. Think about this the next time you hang out with your friend group. Are you guys having meaningful conversations or looking down at your phones most of the time?

One of the last lessons that I learned from doing this was the beauty of being bored. I believe that we should be careful not to eliminate boredom. We have entertainment 24/7 —literally speaking—in our hands. Boredom is the place where ideas happen. It's the place where great conversations take place. It's the place where people can go from one place to another. Think about it: as kids we were oozing with creativity, but that was mostly because we sat around the house at times doing absolutely nothing, which caused us to be inspired to create different kinds of games and acting out a bunch of random scenes.

In 2019 I truly began to live my life in a way that I never thought was possible and it was living in the moment, being intentional and being bored. I ended up finding a love for traveling and that year I went to nine different countries! That's something I never thought was possible or that I would ever do. How?

It began with me running into a friend and having conversations about traveling and how she searches for cheap plane tickets online all the time. Those intentional personal moments helped me connect more with the people around me. She showed me how and I began looking up plane tickets too—it's a fun hobby. One day I was bored—not having social media can do that to you—and so I looked up tickets and found cheap tickets to Europe. And because I had some money saved up, I had just enough to go.

So what is the game plan? How do you move forward? Do you have to give up social media for a year? No. You don't. I would say you don't have to do any of that—though I think it would be cool. But I would suggest just three things.

First, limit your social media use when you are around friends. Try not to pull out your phone around friends but instead try to focus in on the conversation and what is happening. If no one is saying anything, don't pull out your phone, just sit there. Do anything but pull out your phone. Enjoy the company of your friends, because it won't always be there. That's not to say if you want to show them something on your phone, or you are trying to film something. This is more the case of when we are in the company of friends and we just want to scroll on social media or even just sit there texting someone who is not in the room.

Second, allow yourself time to be bored. You hear all the time people say to limit social media, and that doesn't work too well, if we are being honest. Instead what we can do is have times and periods when we are allowing ourselves to be bored. It can be bored Sundays. It can be setting time frames, once a week, twice a week or even more often. It's like the idea of dieting. People think you have to stop eating the junk food, but in reality you just have to start eating healthy food and that will push the junk food out of your diet. You never knew boredom was healthy for you, did you? This isn't saying that you can't do anything. I mean, allow a moment to see what comes to mind, if it has to do with your phone and scrolling it's a no, but if it is something else you want to embark on, go! The more intentional boredom you have, the more adventure you have.

Last, I would suggest that you remember that you will mess up many times—I mean, just writing this chapter I was on my phone until midnight. But the goal isn't to never mess up. The goal is to have a game plan when you do mess up. The goal is to get better and better each day. The goal is to say, "Social media will not control me, but rather I will control social media." When you find yourself slipping in this area, forgive yourself and have a plan to move forward. Create more pockets of bored moments. Hang out with friends and don't take your phone. Do whatever you have to do, but don't give up on being intentional with social media.

I love what it tells us in Proverbs 4:25,26: "Let your eyes look directly forward... ponder the path of your feet." What happens with social media is that we are no longer looking directly forward. We no longer have time or opportunity to ponder the path of our own feet. Meaning? No one is focused on their personal journey. No one is focused on the path God has them on. No one is pondering their path but every moment we are observing someone else's path. Each moment we want to make it look like our path is a certain way. But the call is to focus on where God is taking us and guiding us. The call is to focus on where we are heading.

If we practice this, I will guarantee that we will be getting the most out of college in ways we don't even know! Social media is robbing us of our full college experience. It robs us of being intentional with our friendships. It robs us of the creativity and innovation that we could have. It makes us focus on everyone else's life but our own. If we can say bye to social media, we will be able to say hello to the joys of the college life and more.

Ways to manage your social media

1. Next time you hang out with your friends, try putting away your phone and instead focus on the friends that are around you. *(Endure the awkward silences, the moments when you just want to lift up your phone just out of habit.)*

2. Create moments in your day where you can just be bored, so that you can allow your creative juices to flow. *(This can be you planning to do something on the creative side or just planning to walk around campus allowing yourself to get lost.)*

3. When you go to events on campus, or other things that are happening, be intentional about not being on your phone but instead focus on being connected with what is happening in the moment. *(Avoid being the person who gets on their phone when you feel things get boring and instead be the person who finds ways to get excited about what's going on in the moment.)*

10

Guarding Your Heart

In college there is a topic that we just cannot avoid talking about, relationships. More specifically, romantic relationships. I am not talking about the relationship that your grandma and grandpa have, where they got together as freshmen in high school and remained married. I am talking about the relationship where couples get together their freshman year of college and break up senior year. We all have seen it or maybe we have been in a situation like this. And as much as we don't like to admit it, it hurts no matter what role you are playing. When you break up after years of being with one individual, you start to have this sense of, "I don't know who I am any more without them." This is slightly dangerous to say your senior or junior year of college.

I would love to talk about how being in a romantic relationship is something that should wait until the later portion of your college career—junior or senior year. But if I do that, then no one is really going to read the rest of this chapter. So instead I am going to focus on how to guard your heart if you decide to date. Hopefully that will be more beneficial for you.

A few months after I arrived on the campus of Southwestern Adventist University, I ended up having a really tight group of friends that I hung out with on a regular basis. We hung out on the weekends. We hung out during the week. It was truly the best dream group of friends that you could ask for.

But coming into winter break, things started to change up a little bit. I remember walking into the room where a majority of us were hanging out and someone came up to me and said, "Guess who's interested in each other?" I had a feeling that this was going to take a turn for the worse. And what I later came to find out was that it wasn't just two people interested in each other, but rather several people—within our friend group—who were interested in each other. I knew that from this moment forward, our friend group wouldn't really be the same. Fast-forward several months and people were dating.

What was interesting about this is when you get in a relationship especially as a freshman or sophomore, you have a tendency to want to do everything together. You study together, pray together, make friends together, go to the store together, laugh together, and spend a crazy amount of time together—you get the point. I do want to mention that there is nothing wrong with spending time together. In doing this. what we don't realize is that we are building our lives together when we spend that much time together and never do those things apart from the person we are dating.

Imagine you have building blocks. And you are stacking these blocks on top of each other. You build a nice and solid foundation. After the foundation you build the next layer and so on and so forth until you have this huge pyramid. The way a lot of college students do dating is they enter into a romantic relationship—freshman or sophomore year—and they begin building with their partner, and they haven't even worked on their own foundation, and now they won't, because they are building with someone else. That could be in the area of making friends, your spiritual life, or academics.

For example, your freshman or sophomore year, you may not really know how to make friends. Then you get in a relationship and your partner is the one who knows how to make friends and builds up your friend foundation. A year or two down the line, you break up and now that block that was a foundation for your pyramid gets taken away and you "don't know who you are without them." You don't want to just build your friend foundation through the person you are dating, but you want to be able to build that foundation yourself.

There was a girl, super shy and quiet, but beautiful. She got into a relationship with a very extroverted, popular guy. It was the typical shy girl, extroverted guy relationship. She was a freshman and he was a freshman as well. After dating for three years, she made lots of friends, but the only thing was they weren't necessarily friends that she went out of her way to make, but rather they were friends her boyfriend had that automatically became her friends. There is nothing wrong with that. But coming into their junior year, the relationship started to fall apart, and after they broke up I just remember her saying, "Samson, I don't have any friends at all and I don't know what to do with myself." It makes sense though, because she never had to make friends on her own. Now that was a building block that was taken from her.

So what is the ideal? The ideal is to build your own blocks, not borrow from someone else, but to build your own pyramid. Then when you come across someone, you can put your blocks together, building side-by-side, instead of building on top of each other. You can build a foundation outside of a relationship and in one as well. That way if the time comes when the relationship doesn't work out, then there are no hard feelings. You might be sad that the relationship didn't work out, and that is fine. But you are not going to be in a state where you "don't know who you are."

How do we build our own pyramids? Well, I am glad that you asked. There are topics that every person needs to figure out separately from another human being. And you can be in a relationship and figure it out—but just a heads up, it takes a lot more discipline. Here are some blocks you need to figure out: what you want to do with your life after college(and you can take four years to figure it out, that's okay) how to make friends, study habits, your health, financial stability, and your relationship with God. These are the areas that have the largest effect on couples when the relationship ends. These are the topics that create that "I don't know what to do now" feeling when the relationship is over.

Time and time again, I have run into both girls and guys who fell into the trap of at least two of these and at most all of them. Just imagine, for two years of college you learn how to have a relationship with God with this person. And then for some reason it doesn't work out and now you are left not knowing how to have a relationship with God on your own. We have to guard our hearts and learn how to do these things on our own.

There was a girl and a guy who ended up together their sophomore year. What was beautiful about their relationship was that outside of their relationship, they knew what they wanted to do after college. They learned how to make friends on their own and they did share friends as well. Their health was something they prioritized as individuals, not just as a couple. They both worked on campus jobs and they both had their relationship with God. When they came to realize that they weren't the right one for each other—simply realizing that they were on different paths—they broke up. Neither of them felt lost or confused. I remember the girl saying, "I am going to miss being with him, but I understand it is for the better."

That is the power of building your own blocks! That is the power of guarding your heart. And guess what, if they did end up together, that is only a plus on top of what they have already built. It is almost like you build a pyramid and they build a pyramid and we bring them together. We would have something greater than trying to build something together and getting mad at each other when we threaten to take away pieces.

This is the thing that is amazing: you will always have a richer relationship with someone when you both are able to succeed in each area. Think about it. If one partner is struggling in their relationship with God, because the other partner was strong on their own, they are now able to lift the other up. Same goes for finances, working out, making friends or studying. That is what we call a power couple. There may be one partner who is better than the other in one area, or provides more in one area than the other, but they will be stronger if both parties work towards the same goal. You do your partner a favor by building your own pyramid, by guarding your heart.

There is a Bible verse that I love that goes with this idea of protecting your heart. Proverbs 4:23 says, "Guard your heart above all else, for it determines the course of your life." College is a time when the heart must be guarded the most. It is so easy to feel as though you have wasted your college life because of a relationship. There may be people that you have heard of, maybe situations right now happening around you that are determining the course of lives. You have the chance to protect your life, and that starts by guarding your heart. Guard your heart, and the course of your life—especially college life—will move in a positive direction.

How to guard your heart

1. Whether you met someone before or after college, ask yourself the following questions:

    a. *Do I know how to have a relationship with God outside of this person?*

    b. *Do I know how to make friends outside of this person? Do I even have friends outside of this relationship that I personally formed?*

    c. *Do I rely on this person for going to the gym and taking care of my health?*

    d. *Do I rely on this person for my study habits?*

    e. *Do I rely on this person for my financial stability?*

2. If you said yes to many of the questions in the first part, no worries. The goal is to learn how to do these on your own. And you can take your time. There is no plan for you to break up with your current significant other, so you can take your time.

3. Pick one thing to work on each semester and just seek to grow in that area. *(And by default you will grow your relationship.)*

11

God's Not Toxic

When it comes to spirituality in college, I wish that I could say that I never ran into any trouble. I wish I could say that my walk with God was consistent, and that I never missed a day of devotionals—meaning spending time in prayer and reading the Bible. But that is not the case at all. It was always a battle in college.

My first year in college was the easiest one to maintain my walk with God, especially since I didn't have a lot of friends and I wasn't involved in a lot of things on campus. I didn't have anything that was pulling at my time besides work and school. Something that was also a big help was the time that I spent in a small group on campus where we studied the Bible.

The turn for the worse took place the following semester. I was involved in student government, working the same jobs that I had been working before, and taking classes with a more intense workload. This all played a role in my walk with God declining slowly but surely—I know I was a theology major on my way to becoming a pastor, but my spiritual walk seemed to be in shambles. And this is where God taught me three of my biggest lessons in college when it came to spirituality and walking with Him.

The first lesson is God is not toxic. When you think of your relationship with God, what comes to mind? Do you envision God up in heaven pointing His finger like a frustrated parent, saying, "You better spend time with Me." And then when you don't, do you envision Him giving you the cold shoulder throughout the day? Feelings of guilt, sadness, and possibly disappointment?

When we talk about God not being "toxic," what we are referring to is whether someone is toxic in a relationship. A toxic person is usually being unreasonable. This idea of being toxic in a relationship could come from many directions, but the direction that we are going to go is in the area of demanding your time, asking for something. This can be asking for you to cut yourself off from your parents. Asking you to cut yourself off from your friends. Asking you to cut yourself off from your school and your career. All simply for the reason of spending time with that person. That is toxic. And why do we have a similar image when it comes to our relationship with God?

The thing that helped me so much is recognizing that God is not toxic. He is understanding. He knows that you have fifteen exams coming up and that you also have to work, and that you are also part of a club. He understands the importance of community and hanging out with your friends and staying connected to family. He understands all of that. He isn't demanding you to give the most amount of time to Him and Him alone.

There were days my second year in college where I would be running around from what literally felt like right when I woke up until about 10 at night. I was going from meeting to class to class to meeting to studying to work to studying—and hopefully finding

food in there somewhere. I would feel guilty and
ashamed for not spending the time I spent with Him the
year prior. But we have to realize that God understands.
Like seriously, He does. He understands the seasons
that we are in, currently. There might have been
seasons when you had time, use them wisely, but there
will be other seasons when you have less time, and God
sees that.

The second lesson is if you don't learn to spend
time with Him in college, it will not be a priority when
you leave. Okay, I know I am going to sound like I am
going back on myself here, but follow me. Yes, it is true
that God is not toxic demanding our time, but that does
not mean that we shouldn't try everything in our power
to connect with Him in different ways.

Trying to spend time with God my second year in
college was crazy! It was like trying to fit a thread
through the eye of a needle. One time coming back from
a meeting and starting to work on homework, I felt
overwhelmed and tired and almost like I couldn't go
forward. It was in that moment that I remembered I
hadn't read the Bible that day. So before I began my

homework, I opened up the Bible and just read a passage. I can't remember what verse it was that I read, but I remember being lifted up with a new energy.

Was it the passage that did it? I am not quite sure, but one thing I know is that it was a breath of fresh air. If I had to compare it to something, I would compare it to finding a moment in the day to connect with your best friend. Have you ever had that moment when you felt overwhelmed and you just ran into your best friend? There is this feeling of relief, maybe a laugh about something that happened that day, maybe an opportunity to rant or maybe you just sit there and your presence for each other gives you that breath of fresh air. God is a friend in the same way. It's the relationships in college where people were intentional that ended up following me out of college.

I knew that God wasn't toxic, but that didn't mean I didn't need to value Him. It didn't mean that I didn't have to strive to make Him a part of my day. College schedules can get clogged up with a lot of stuff. But the reality is that we shouldn't feel like God is toxic. We can be excited that God understands our situations and that He is rooting for us to do well. But at the same time, we still should value Him, and we still can value Him by finding ways to spend time with Him and connect with Him.

The third lesson is we need Him. When it comes to making friends, we need Him. When it comes to passing classes, we need Him. When it comes to our romantic relationships, we need Him—though we may think we have this one in the bag. When it comes even to our health, finances and future plans, we need Him.

I remember I had a huge math test that was coming up and I was planning on getting in a couple of good study sessions before the test. The a few days before the test came around, I did a devotional that focused on obedience to our parents. When I came to the end of that, I told God, "Whatever my parents ask me to do, I will value it." Be careful what you pray for, they say. Next minute, my mom was asking me to do everything under the sun! I found myself having a very, very small study session that night, not enough to count.

The next day my dad does the same. My dad called on me to do this, that, and the third thing. I didn't know if this was a test from God or if I was testing God myself. The day of the test comes and I get asked to take my aunt to a town forty-five minutes away from where we lived, but because of my schedule I politely declined. Which felt like it gave me a break, until they told me the time. It was just early enough to make it to my class. So I took my aunt and got to school with no time to study. After getting to the classroom, we had about ten minutes before the class started. I tried to get some help from a friend who was explaining something we needed to know for the test, but all I could think about was how I didn't do my devotional that morning. So I sat in class and did my devotional. I had one friend who said, "Dude, are you reading the Bible? You should be studying." But I had given up.

Once the test was handed out I was sad, because I looked down at the test paper and I knew absolutely nothing! Can you imagine that? But I prayed and told God, "I am going to put down an answer for every question." And that's what I did. I was the last to finish and as I turned in my test, I remember just telling the teacher, "Sorry about my test, I will do better next time."

After a few days I went back into the teacher's office to talk to him about why I did so poorly. And he pulled out my test and started grading it, right in front of me. He just kept laughing, saying, "You think you failed." I thought I might have gotten a D or a C on it. When he passed it back to me, all I saw was 101 percent. I nearly cried. But that is what I am trying to say, we need God. I have experienced countless stories where God came through for me regarding classes, work, student government and even friends and family. WE NEED GOD!

This is like the secret sauce to getting the most you can out of college. Literally, the relationship with God is something that has amplified my college experience and that is because we need God to have what they call "good success."

When you begin, it becomes fun to try to implement a relationship with God in everything you do, from something simple like praying before homework to praying while walking on campus. There were also times when I got a chance to have date sessions with God. A date with God was just me and God hanging out, going to a coffee shop or going to eat. Taking the Bible with me, or even a journal and just talking with Him. The biggest thing is not to beat yourself up if your devotional life doesn't look like it did before, because God isn't beating you up.

And get this, coming around to my senior year in college, my strong devotional life came back. For some reason, senior theology majors have a little more free time in their schedule—I'm not sure who set this up but I love it! Over the summer there was a lot that happened—I'll go over that in a later chapter—that seemed to put a strain on my relationship with God. But being able to see that God isn't toxic, that He is a friend and also the reality that I needed Him helped me maintain and even grow in our relationship.

My professors required us to have a devotional every day and that was a part of our grade. That was a huge game-changer for me, because it felt like I got to go back to my freshman year, when I had that consistent morning devotional. Not only that, but because I had more free time my senior year, I also had the chance to have a nighttime devotional with my roommate Edgar

Restrepo—some of my best nights came from those night devotionals. My busy schedule was just the season that I was in at the time. I could have been a lot more patient with myself.

When it comes to the idea of maintaining spirituality—a relationship with God—it is just like maintaining a relationship with a friend. Friends understand when you get busy. They would never judge. But friends do feel extra valued when you value them, especially in the midst of a busy schedule. When you show them how important they are in your life. and if your friend would get excited at you showing your love and devotion to them, how much more the One who died for you? That is a beautiful thought: "I can get God excited by showing Him love in my busy schedule." Also, know that God looks at you and says, "you are enough for Me." You are enough for God, just you in the midst of your schedule—let that sink in for a minute. Now, the real question is; can we say the same thing about God? Can we say, "God you are enough for me."

If you can maintain spirituality in college, then you can really do it anywhere. Your college years can be some of your most busiest times—until marriage and kids, of course—but you can get excited that you don't serve a toxic God. And because we don't, we need to simply find ways to value Him because the reality is we need Him!

How to maintain spirituality

1. Ask yourself, how do you view God in your college experience? Demanding of your time?
2. Understand that God is not demanding of your time, but at the same time we need Him for everything that we do and we should value Him.
3. What are ways we can show we value God?
    a. *Having dates scheduled with God after super-busy weeks.*
    b. *Prayer walks between classes, where you just share with God about your day.*
    c. *Embracing whatever time you do spend with Him each day.*
4. What are ways you can involve God knowing that you need Him for everything you do?
    a. *Including Him in your study time through worship music or prayer.*
    b. *Including Him in your relationship with devotionals with your significant other.*
    c. *Including Him in your work simply by relying on Him for each project and assignment.*

12

Learn How to Fail

Going into my junior year, I thought that I had everything a college student could ask for. I had all A's all throughout my time at Southwestern. I was involved in student government. I was developing a nice close friend group. And things were starting to move for me in ways that I didn't imagine.

I didn't want to just stop there—as I wouldn't want to recommend anyone else to do. Coming into the spring semester of my junior year, there was a girl—there is always a girl, right?—that I was interested in for a long time. She didn't attend the university; I just happened to know her through a family friend. During that semester I had "confessed love to her"—basically I told her I liked her—and she felt the same way. Now anyone that has liked anyone, if they ever told you that they liked you back, you know that it's an amazing feeling! But sadly, as this chapter is about failing, it didn't work out. About a month later she told me, "Sorry, I actually started talking to someone three days after you told me you liked me." I thought that was crazy! I was hurt, as anyone else would be—I didn't even make it a month, struggles. But in my mind, I was able to brush it off because I felt like I had bigger fish to fry.

You see, there was another position that I wanted to run for in student leadership. There was an association of student government presidents from different universities in North America, and we would meet together once a year. I felt this burning desire to run for the position. I was super excited for all the things that I wanted to do and implement. What made me excited was the idea of truly being involved on a more national level and making impact in all the universities.

I ended up running for the position and I thought I had done everything as correctly as possible, but I ended up losing in the end—by one vote might I add. Is that petty to say? I remember leaving that place rethinking life, asking myself the question of what could I have done differently. Imagine, you are going for something that you feel even God is behind you in and then all of a sudden it doesn't happen? With everyone from my school supporting me, I felt like I had let them all down. But I decided to brush it off because, once again, I felt like I had bigger fish to fry.

With the school year winding down, we wanted to end the school year on a good note, just like any student government would, right? One of the last events that took place on our campus was roller-skating, super fun and exciting. But towards the end of the night, I got a little excited doing tricks on the skates and I ended up breaking my leg. It was hard on us as a student government, because I was in charge of the end-of-year events that took place on the last week of school. But instead I spent the rest of the year and part of the summer on drugs and in a cast. Bye-bye end of the year. And this was especially hard for me because I had interest in joining the basketball team for the university the following year. But after this situation, I knew that there were no chance.

Whew, okay. You made it through the sob stories, now for the lessons. During those last few weeks of school and even going into the summer, I felt those were some of the darkest times of my life. From the possible relationship that ended, to not getting the position I felt called to, to breaking my leg and not ending on the note I thought we'd end on, it all put me in a dark spot. Sometimes we can get so caught up in the wins that come our way, that when losing happens it kills us. I wasn't in a great position, but more blessings happened to me than failures in my college experience.

I share these stories and I write this chapter to help you realize something I wish I could have heard during that time. I took so many risks that year. I risked running for a position that I had no idea what it all entailed. I risked pushing for a service day that I didn't even know how it was going to go. And everything turned out amazing! But I also risked talking to a girl, which did not work out and ended up being a blessing— because instead I got my wife!! I love you, Natali

Sembeba. I risked running for the position, and it was a blessing I didn't get that position, because I wouldn't have experienced some of the beauty of my senior year—which I talk more of in the next chapter. And even the broken leg was a blessing. If I had not broken my leg, I don't think I would have been as financially literate—I ended up watching a lot of YouTube, and I ran across a financial video that made me take care of my finances.

Life is really interesting because your failures can easily become some of your greatest success stories. I am here to tell you that you can't wait for someone to come into your life and make you think positively. I was on the couch in my apartment and my roommates tried to encourage me, but they were not in my head, they were not in those moments. I had to see it for myself. They can try to help open my eyes, but at the end of the day, I am the one that opens my eyes. Only I could do that. And only you can do that for yourself.

The Bible tells us that "the eye is the widow to the heart." Whatever the eye (window) focuses on, that will be the condition of the body. If the eye is placed in a location of light, the whole body will be filled with light. If the eye is placed in a location of darkness, the whole body will be filled with darkness. Where does your eye focus? The positive in life? Or the negative? Whatever you focus on, that will be the flow of your life.

In this book, I am calling you to do a lot. From being uncomfortable so others can be comfortable, to experimenting, to reaching out to mentors, it can all be intimidating, especially if you run into moments where you fail and where you make mistakes. But you can't let the places where you fall cause you to get down in the dumps like I did. I challenge you to focus on the positive. I challenge you to see through the failures and look for the success.

The more that you attempt something in life, the more likely you will run into failure. Imagine you shoot ten free-throws, and you make ten out of ten. That is really good, but if you sit there and shoot one hundred shots, you may eventually miss a shot. And if you shoot one thousand shots you will miss, a lot. Failure comes with trying out new things, and the secret to making it past the failure is letting your eye focus on the positive instead of the negative.

Many of you reading this haven't started college yet or you might just be getting started. Either way, I challenge you, when struggles come your way on your journey to getting the most out of college, not to focus on the failures but focus beyond them. Learn from them, grow from them, count the little victories, focus on the positive and you will be surprised by how things turn around. Maybe next week, maybe next month, and maybe even next year, but eventually you will see it!

How to fail

1. We forget many times that the moments where we fail are some of the best lessons we can learn from, more than the success.

2. What connections were made in the process of failing? *(There are people that you met, whether it was a deep relationship formed or just a moment, that may be used in the future.)*

3. If you had a chance to do it again, do you have ways to do it better or differently? Yes. You've now gained the knowledge needed to do better when you get the next chance.

4. Even when you fail at something, you have knowledge about the campus or the project that you didn't have before. You are able to share your ideas with someone because you have had experience in that area.

5. Think about the good that can come from something not working out, and the blessings that are ahead of you. *(Positive thinking can go a long way towards encouraging you to keep going and to not be afraid to try again.)*

13

The Conversation that Changed My Life

During my last year at Southwestern Adventist University, I had the opportunity to work in the advancement office for the school—something I did my junior year as well.

While working for the advancement office, we did an off-campus fundraiser event and I had an opportunity to meet one of my boss's friends, Melody Ginnetti. She is a licensed clinical social worker who worked with a lot of people through counselling and therapy. Now before I go any further, I would like to mention that before meeting her, I always had the understanding that counselling or really any type of therapy was for people who were really struggling! I

imagined it being for people who really, really need it. I
thought it to be a last resort. I grew up with the
mentality that if you have any problems, take them to
Jesus. He will handle all your situations. But on that day
my perspective changed.

On the drive back to campus after the event, I
had the chance to sit next to her in the back seat. I had
the chance to get to know her a little bit and learn more
about her work and what she does. During the
conversation, she asked me, "Have you ever been
counselled or gone to therapy before?" My response
was, "No, I never had to." That's where I messed up. She
began asking me what I meant and then she told me
something that I never will forget. "Going to counselling
is like going to the doctor, or like going to the dentist. it
is a checkup for the way you think." She continued to
explain how it can be help prevent problems, just like
preventive care for your body and your teeth.

I entertained the thought and decided I was
going to keep the conversation going. I asked her, "Okay,
I just 'signed up' for your counselling session and I have
no idea what to talk about, where would we start?" She

just began asking me some really basic questions on life and it got deeper and deeper as we went on. By the end of the two-hour car ride, I was convinced that I had to try a counselling session.

You see, the truth is, throughout my life I had been wrestling with thoughts in my head and I always imagined I had to fight them on my own. What I think of myself, what I think of others, entering college for the first time, dealing with success, dealing with failure, handling a break-up or even handling a new relationship. There are things that you are experiencing right now, and you are developing a way of thinking around it. And the way that we think at many times can be very wrong, but by letting someone in there, those thoughts get challenged and improved. And that is what she showed me that day.

Moving forward, I told myself that I wanted to try counselling in some form. I began talking to faculty at my school, finding ways for me to get involved in it. After a while I got connected with a counselor and had my first session. What was so amazing about it was for the first time in my life, I had given someone the uncut, real version of my life story, something I had never done before. Just the honest raw thought process of my life events. And not just that, but I had input from someone who gave me amazing feedback.

One of the things that she challenged me to do was to write down the names of a few people I would tell my struggles to and I did. Then later down the road she encouraged me actually to share with them those struggles. She emphasized the importance of being more transparent with my close friends. As I began the journey of sharing with my close friends about my struggles, I began to experience more and more victory over the very things I felt were polluting my mind. What was cool was that as I opened up more with my close friends, they opened up more with me.

What that counselling taught me was the beauty of community and transparency. I don't think I would have succeeded in anything out of college without community and transparency. I don't think this book would have been written properly without community and transparency.

The lesson that I am calling for you to receive from this chapter is simple but hard. The lesson is to take advantage of counselling while you are in college. A lot of colleges offer free counselling services to their students—take advantage of it!

Your greatest thinking happens in college. You are chewing on a lot when it comes to friendships, relationships, how you work, how you think, how you treat yourself, and even how you treat others. You deal with how you will handle success and failure. Would you rather learn about all this, ten years into your career, or would you rather learn about it in college where you can work on it and even—like me—learn it right before you go into your career. Learn in a place where you can have mentors supporting you. You are in the perfect position as a college student to learn about yourself. You will be blown away by how much it helps you.

My first year working as a pastor, I felt like I was in one of the greatest situations I could have been in. I came into the church understanding how I am not as transparent as I thought I was, how I was not an authentic person. Coming into pastoral ministry with that understanding helped me to be intentional about being transparent about being authentic. And that translated into other areas in my life—friendships, relationships, even with my family. What do you struggle with? Do you know? What stops you from doing some counselling?

Whatever you are facing or have faced in your life, there is no reason that you should be facing it alone. We were not meant for that. The Bible tells us, "It is not good for man to be alone." This is not just speaking about marriage, but about the aspect of community. Whether something happened or you feel like nothing happened, it's not good for you to be alone in the way that you think and process life. Everyone needs a different perspective, someone to bring in their two cents. We need each other.

Now with every major life change that takes place, I try to do a few sessions of counselling to process it, and it has always been worth it—even though it isn't free like it used to be in college. None of us are perfect in the way we think. And even if we feel as though we are perfect, there is one thing that we cannot get from ourselves and that is a different perspective. I do want to say that some people go the route of reading self-development books and that is beneficial, but there is a bigger benefit from processing thoughts with another human being who can respond more directly to you.

I do want to mention that it isn't easy finding someone you can relate to when it comes to counselling. That is a process that may require a level of patience. You may have to try a different counselor, and that is okay. I am convinced that if you are willing to work on the way you think about counselling, it will come back to benefit you in an amazing way and trust me, people around you will notice.

Connecting with a counselor

1. Many colleges offer free counselling centers. This is a great place to start when it comes to looking for a counselor.

2. There are a lot of online services where people can connect with counselors. *(My first recommendation is in person, but online is better than having no options.)*

3. Connect with friends and family who have gone to counselling and see who they use. *(They are already connected with someone who is helping them, so you might be able to connect well with them too.)*

4. Remember, when you are more transparent in the counselling sessions, the more you will get out of it. *(When you hold back, or even lie, counselling no longer can serve you.)*

14

What's Your Plan After Graduation?

When we think of graduation, we think of arriving somewhere. Don't get me wrong, arriving somewhere is very much what it is—trust me, before college the last time I properly graduated was kindergarten. Graduation is a glorious day. You think of all that it will take, or has taken, to get there. You think about the fact that some of your family never reached this point and you have made it and are going to make it. But if in the end all we get is a degree—a piece of paper—would it really have been worth it? Maybe if you are going to the medical field or the engineering world there is a plus, but outside of that, what really would be the point?

When it comes to graduation, people get really nervous. There seems to always be one question that gets graduates really nervous and that is, "What are you doing after graduation?" Now, if you are starting off the school year as a freshman or sophomore, you haven't gotten that question yet—but probably some have gotten it in high school. But I want to let you know that question is just as important your freshman year in college as it is in your senior year. So, I ask you. What is your plan after graduation?

College is the perfect place to come in order to figure out the answer to that question. *Well, that was a common-sense answer*, you might think. But what seems to happen a lot is students go through college expecting the teacher to tell them the answer one day or expecting it to fall into their lap one day—and getting a job isn't the answer either. When their senior year comes, the question gets asked, "What are your plans after graduation?" And fear strikes!

This question may not get fully answered until you graduate, and the ironic thing is that it may even come after graduation. But what matters most is not when it comes but rather getting the answer in bits and pieces along the journey. The real question that we should be asking ourselves is, "What difference do you want to make in the world?" The first question implies you can't do anything until you get the degree, but the second question implies that you can begin right now. So, I ask the question again, "What difference do you want to make in the world?"

If you are lost, start with passions that you have, they can be different than your major, because maybe you are called to combine them somehow. A friend from SWAU had a passion for art, but her major was biology. So instead of picking one direction she decided that she was going to mix the two and do art for biology books. How amazing, right? And I remember on one occasional a student on campus was preaching a sermon about the heart. During the message, he had her come up while he was preaching, and she painted an art piece of the heart.

A lot of the time we think we have to pick, but no, we don't. So, I ask the question again: What difference do you want to make in the world? What movement do you want to be a part of? Do you want to change the world in a specific way? I believe that if you want to change the world, you can start with a campus. And if you can change a campus, then you can change a town. And if you can change a town, then you can change a state, and if you can change a state, you then can change a country. If you can change a country, then you can change the world.

What's the answer to the question, "What are your plans after graduation?" Changing the world, that's the answer. And how are you going to do that? That's the point of college. College prepares you. College gives you the opportunities that you need. College sets you up. College is that beginning place you go to in order to make that difference. How are you going to spend your time in college? How have you spent your time in college? Enjoy it and make good use of it. It doesn't matter the school that you are at, but rather what matters is the choice that you make. What matters is when you see your campus, are you willing to make a difference there, and allow it to transfer over to your career and the rest of your life?

When I came into college, I was nervous and I thought that it was going to be a fail—and they were many times when I failed, but it always worked out. I thought that there was no way that I was going to make an impact. But college showed me all the tools that I needed in order to change the world. College got me connected with all the right mentors that have helped me along the way. College was the soil that gave me all the nutrients that I needed in order to grow and make that difference. What about you? What's your plan after graduation?

How to get prepared for graduation

1. Be patient with yourself. Understand that you have the next four years to answer the question, so take it year by year.

2. Starting with what difference you want to make in the world may seem overwhelming. Try thinking instead what difference you want to make on your campus. Or on an even smaller scale, in your department? *(When you see that you can make a difference on a small level, you will gain the confidence you need to make a difference on a bigger level.)*

3. Surround yourself with the mentors to help you answer this question. You will be surprised by how much they want to help you figure out that answer.

4. Don't be afraid. The Bible has the phrase "Don't be afraid" 365 times. When you decide to do something, know that you walk with the Creator God Who will supply all your needs.

What to Do Next?

1. Next time you walk on your campus, implement something that you learned. Literally, just take it one lesson at a time. Don't feel like you must do everything at once. Remember you have a few years to get the most out of your experience. Take on only what you can handle.

2. Don't be afraid of making mistakes, but rather have fun with it. Making mistakes is a part of the process of making an impact.

3. Trust God.

4. When you graduate or even before that, I challenge you to pass this book on to a freshman. Share with them your experience with this book and with college. Empower the next generation.

5. Support students like you, who want to get the most out of college, by giving to a scholarship set-up at Southwestern Adventist University. Whether it is a dollar or thousand, let's work together in helping students succeed. The *More Than A Degree Scholarship* can be found at: swau.edu/morethanadegree

Endowment

Thank you for purchasing this book. 20% of the profits from this book will go to the "More Than A Degree" Scholarship Endowment at Southwestern Adventist University to help students like Samson, who sought to earn more than a degree.

Samson Sembeba

Join The Mission – Equipping Young Adults

This book is also part of talks and workshops on leadership. Please share this book with your school or church administration. We would love to do an in-person/virtual workshop at your school both high school and college or church or ministry.

Let's Host a Leadership Workshop Today

For more information or to support this mission, visit our website: samsonsembeba.com
Samson Sembeba Email: ssembeba@gmail.com